FULTON J. SHEEN
Our Grounds for Hope

FULTON J. SHEEN

Our Grounds for Hope

Enduring Words of Comfort and Assurance

Foreword by Msgr. Eugene V. Clark

Resurrection Press
An Imprint of
CATHOLIC BOOK PUBLISHING CO.
Totowa • New Jersey

Resurrection Press edition published February, 2000 by
special arrangement with the Estate of Fulton J. Sheen.
Previously published as *Lenten & Easter Inspirations* and *Cross-Ways*.

Resurrection Press, Ltd.
P.O. Box 248
Williston Park, NY 11596

ISBN 1-878718-56-8

Library of Congress Catalog Card Number 99-75980

Cover design and photography by John Murello.
Photos in text by John Murello.

Printed in Canada.

1 2 3 4 5 6 7 8 9 0

Foreword

THIS PUBLICATION OF THE THOUGHTS AND ADVICE of Archbishop Fulton J. Sheen will, I expect, prove wonderfully popular and rewarding.

Writing and speaking to millions of people is a phenomena of our era. As you know, Archbishop Sheen with his fine mind and his exceptional doctorate in philosophy learned how to bring his careful clear counseling to millions — first in radio and then in television.

But there is more here than a good thinker speaking. His luminous delivery and his goodness and charm — not to mention those eyes — were gifts that few others could sustain in broadcast. Spiritual advice and encouragement had mainly been a one-on-one conversation between director and aspirant. A few like the great Athanasius, Ambrose and Chrysostom; and then Dominic and Bossuet and Ronald Knox held audiences fixed by a rich understanding of man and the action of grace on him.

The special genius — which you will find in this book — turned broadcast into a personal conversation on the elements of the Christian life. The perceptive Archbishop was so clear and indeed compelling in his spiritual advice that incredible numbers of people accepted his message as personal to them; and indeed it was. Others, we pray the Lord, will be given similar gifts and develop them as he did for the good of the people.

What could not be incorporated in the text of this book are the careful, two-second pauses after each thought he delivered, allowing us to make the sentiment ours. The world is full of people whose lives were turned around spiritually by the words of their beloved Fulton J. Sheen. He was — and there are few competitors — the most popular, esteemed and "listened to" priest in the history of the Catholic Church in the United States.

The guidance that you will find in this book will refresh your memory of the power of Archbishop Sheen's clear thoughts and deep, personal spirituality. We thank and congratulate the publisher.

Monsignor Eugene V. Clark

Christic the Victim

NEVER BE DISCOURAGED. You do not have the power to relieve yourself of sorrow or grief or pain. But Our Lord did on the Cross. He could have turned the crown of thorns into a garland of rosebuds, and the nails into scepters, and the tattered rags of His Flesh into the robe of coronation. He was tempted to short en His agony, as those at the foot of the Cross taunted:

> "Let the Christ, the King of Israel, come
> down, now from the Cross, that we may
> see and believe."
>
> MARK 15:32

But he did not come down. It is human to come down, but it is divine to hang there. The priest, once he begins the Mass, which is the Memorial of Calvary, is not permitted to interrupt it. He must finish it, as Our Lord finished His Redemption on the Cross. Your race is nearly run. Courage! Hope! Joy! Remember that He, Who has passed through Calvary and Gethsemane, is at your side, cheering you to victory.

"Do not think that because I said, 'Take up your cross daily and follow Me' that I give you not a peace which surpasses all understanding. Remember that I, Who told My Apostles to take up the Cross, took them aside into the desert to rest awhile and prepared a feast for them by the lakeside, gave them the wine gift at the marriage feast, multiplied bread and fish in their hands and showed them on Easter that the Cross was the prelude to the Glorified Body."

The Crucifiers

"And now Judas, His betrayer, was full of
        remorse at seeing Him condemned,
so that he brought back to the chief priests
        and elders their thirty pieces of silver;
        'I have sinned,' he told them,
'in betraying the blood of an innocent
        man.'
'What is that to us?' they said. 'It concerns
        thee only.'"

MATTHEW 27:3-4

When We Cannot Pray

SOMETIMES A SOUL IS UNABLE TO PRAY when in pain. This does not mean that it is any less attached to God. It must be remembered that when we are well, we very often have a sensible feeling of our devotion and love of God. When we come closer to God, this sensible feeling leaves us and we are joined more to God, not by the interior or the exterior senses of the lower part of our soul but by pure Spirit.

> Consecrate these trials of my life which
>   would go unrewarded unless united
>   with Thee:
> transubstantiate me, so that like bread
>   which is now Thy Body
> and wine which is now Thy Blood,
> I too may be wholly Thine.
> The Substance of my Life, my soul, my
>   mind, my will, my heart —
> transubstantiate them, transform them
>   wholly into Thy service,
> so that through me all may know how
>   sweet is the love of Christ.

Christ Suffers in You

Jesus is not just your Exemplar
As the model to the canvas.
He is not like oil on your baptismal water,
But like a blood transfusion in your veins,
Like the sunlight dancing in a stained-glass Gothic,
Like the fragile glass that breaks in sympathy
With the vibrant chords of a twin harmony.

He does not send your pain:
He sends it to Himself
As the mother tastes the bitter draught
Before passing it to childish lips.

So long as you think of Christ outside your aches,
As the book of consolation that you read,
Or the healing medicine on the shelf,
You will never be a part of the saving Cross.

Does not even the gutter's stained drop
Reflect the brightness of the distant sun
And is not its inner self lifted to the sun,
Leaving only the scum behind?

In some such way,
Those whose pains are like moisture
Are absorbed into the world's redemption
And those whose hearts are as mud
Only harden with the fires of love.

We all weep that Jesus had no inn,
But today, does not Jesus weep
Because so few give Him neither inn nor Cross?

Jesus is never off His Cross!
He left it not in challenge:
"Come down! We will believe,"
But what is harder than to hang there
Is to believe that He hangs on me.

What Has to Be Added to Suffering?

WHAT IS THE EXTRA INGREDIENT in suffering — which when absent prompts a curse and when present becomes a joy?

You must unite your sufferings and sorrows with Christ and see your Calvary as coming from the Hand of God. Our Lord saw the Cup of His Passion as given to Him, not by Judas or Pilate or Caiphas or the people but by His Father: "Shall I not drink the Cup My Father Himself has appointed for Me?" Pain without Christ is suffering; pain with Christ is sacrifice.

It is hard for us to see in the accidents and trials of life, in sickness, in bereavement, in financial loss, in cancerous bodies and leprous limbs, any Divine Purpose. That is why Our Blessed Lord had to take suffering upon Himself, in order to show us that it is the Father's Cup.

"It is the Lord that speaks....
'I, the Fashioner of darkness, the Creator of
     light,

> I, the Maker of peace, the Author of
>   calamity.
> I, the Lord, am the Doer of all this.'"

ISAIAH 45:7

Every tear, disappointment and grieved heart is a blank check. If we write our name on it, it is worthless. If we sign it with Christ's Name, it is infinite in its value. In prosperity, Christ gives you His gifts; in suffering with faith, He gives you Himself.

Complicity

Feel a self-reproachful complicity
In every crime on page one.
Feel every man's sin as your own
As a mother feels a daughter's pains.
Take another's sickness unto your own
As "He bore our infirmities."

Against a wall with arms outstretched
A wife in sobbing tears dost fling herself
At the husband's tale of another woman
And he at the sight of it did say:
"At that moment I saw Christ hanging on the Cross."
The lesser cross revealed the greater Cross,
In which Love is wounded by our sins.

Only the wounded know how to bind up wounds:
The converted sinner has more mercy than the
        sinless Pharisee;
True helpers are those who have been bombed out.
Hence, He, in the words of Scripture,
"Has compassion on our infirmities."

You are not alone! You are on a team!
Hurt, they carry you to the sidelines.
"Why should this happen to me?" you ask —
Forgetful that you helped the team to win.
No suffering is wasted!
As clouds carry rain over mountains,
So your patience with cancer,
Your resignation to withered limbs,
Rebounds to some soul in Ceylon
And helps a missionary in Seoul.

The greatest tragedy is not what people suffer
But that they have no one whom they love
To whom they can offer their cross.
This is wasted pain —
The pain of the Cross, not the Crucifix;
The guillotine, not the oneness with Christ.

Good Friday:
Enemies Too Optimistic

THE ENEMIES OF OUR BLESSED LORD were too optimistic on Good Friday. Thanks to mass propaganda and organized demonstrations before a governor's palace, they convinced a timesaving politician that "We shall not have this man rule over us." When finally they reduced Him to a common criminal, they hurled four taunts at Him on the Cross, boasts about their victory and His defeat. First, He said that He would "destroy the Temple and then rebuild it;" but the Temple was still standing as a reproach to His boastfulness. Second, "He saved others, but now could not save Himself." Third, He said He was a King, but He was proven to be a mock King, with a crown of thorns for a diadem, a nail for a scepter, blood for royal purple, a Crucifixion for a coronation. Finally, His claim that He was the Son of God was now a stupid lie, for if He was, why did not God deliver Him?

When He is taken down from the Cross, Joseph of Arimathea boldly goes to Pilate to ask for the Body of

Our Lord. The Greek word which the gospel says Joseph used was *soma*, which is the word of respect for a body. Pilate was too optimistic that the power of Caesar would no longer be challenged and he told Joseph that he would give him not the *soma* but the *ptoma*, which means cadaver or rubbish. The final optimism of the enemies was the setting of the guards, not to prevent the Resurrection but to prevent the Apostles from stealing the Body and saying He had risen from the dead. Finally, they rolled a great stone in front of His tomb. This was the final victory! He who had called Himself "the Rock" is not rockbound in a tomb — never to rise again. Even before Nietzsche wrote his blasphemous lines, the enemies had scored that apparent victory, for God is dead.

Good Friday: Friends Too Pessimistic

ON THE OTHER HAND, the friends of Our Lord were too pessimistic and despairing. Though they had heard Our Lord say that He would rise from the dead after being in the belly of the earth for three days, they still did not believe. The women go to the grave on Easter morning with spices which they had prepared, not to greet a Risen Lord but to anoint a dead body. Not in the least expecting the Resurrection, they ask: "Who will roll us back the stone from the door of the sepulcher?" Mary Magdalene herself, who had risen from the deadness of sin into the newness of Divine Life and who had heard Our Lord say that He was the Resurrection and the Life, came also with spices and weeping, not with joy in anticipation of a Resurrection but with sorrow, for the Beloved was dead.

When Magdalene finds the tomb empty, instead of believing that He has risen, she says to the Angel who asks her why she weeps: "Because they have taken away My Lord and I know not where they have laid

Him." When Our Lord finally appears before her in the garden, she does not even look up. Seeing a figure whom she mistakes for a gardener, she calls Our Lord "sir" and asks: "If thou hast taken Him hence, tell me where thou hast laid Him and I will take Him away." She is not prepared to face one who conquers death, but rather to find the corpse and rebury it. Finally, Our Lord speaks to her and she recognized Him, saying now not "sir" but *"Raboni!* (Master!)." She runs to tell Peter and John, saying "I have seen the Lord." But they, hearing it, do not believe it, saying it is a woman's tale.

The Worst Thing Evil Can Do

WHEN, AT ONE MOMENT, I see a naked criminal on the gallows, forsaken by followers, rejected by the dominant spiritual forces of His time, condemned by the state whose name stands in all history as the synonym for human law; when three days later I hear an Angel say to a woman in search of a grave, "Why seek you the living with the dead?" (Luke 24:5); when I hear Him, as the Divine Stranger on a roadway Easter afternoon, say to His companions: "Ought not Christ to have suffered these things and so to enter into His glory?" (Luke 24:26); when I see Him, Who had been nailed, walking in the newness of life in the clouds of the morning — then I begin to understand that since evil could never do anything worse than crucify Goodness, it could never be truly victorious again. Conquered in its full armor and in the moment of its monumental momentum, evil might in the future win some battles, but it would always lose the war. Evil is more powerful than goodness when the battlefield is the physical, as a Niagara Falls can sweep a good man to his destruction; nevertheless, goodness is more powerful than evil when the issue is spiritual, for as the mind of man can harness the destructive forces of a Niagara, so the Goodness of God can let evil do its mightiest, which is to crucify Divine Life and still conquer it by rising, not with Wounds but with glorious Scars on Hands and Feet and Side.

From that day on, all the darkness in the world cannot put out the light of a single candle. All the swords of earth cannot kill the life of a single immortal soul. All the evil in the universe cannot black out the fixed flash of that instant and intolerant enlightenment — the Lightning made eternal as the Light. No one therefore shall take away our hope for any person or nation, regardless of the passing forces of evil.

Sympathy

NO ONE CAN EVER PASS ON TO ANOTHER the comfort that God gives until he has himself felt it after a moment of trial and suffering. Never seek true wisdom from a person who has never suffered. He can give advice, but he can give no consolation. He can explain, but he cannot solace. Our Blessed Lord told Peter after he had fallen and come back again to the Master that he would be the strength of his fellow Apostles.

To feel lonely and solitary in pain is to forget that it can profit others when it is put into the scarred Hands of Christ. No one is lonely except he who is self-centered and who cuts himself off from communion with his fellow man. A modern dramatist, who already lives a lonely hell within himself, has written a description of three people in hell. All are in a room that has no exit. They are incapable of community or talking to one another or of telling their distress to one another. This is hell. But the saint knows that just as he could bring "bread" to the hungry if he were well, so he can bring the merits of his sufferings to another, even when he cannot go to them. On Judgment Day it will be found that those who have communicated the merits of their pains to other souls on this earth will be credited with a greater ransom than missionaries.

> "God, harden me against myself,
> This coward with pathetic voice,
> Who craves for ease and rest and joy.
> Myself, arch-traitor to myself,
> My hollowest friend, my deadliest foe,
> My clod whichever way I go.
> Yet One there is can curb myself
> Can roll the strangling load from me,
> Break off the yoke and set me free."
>
> CHRISTINA ROSSETTI

We all need sympathy, but we must avoid morbidly seeking for it. The search for sympathy fixes in our minds — as certain chemicals fix the photographic negative — the permanent impression which we hold of ourselves as persons needing sympathy, that is, as weak persons.

Empty and Full

THE LAST WORDS OF MARY that were spoken in Sacred Scripture were the words of total abandonment to the will of God. "Whatsoever He shall say to you, that do ye." As Dante said: "In His will is our peace." Love has no other destiny than to obey Christ. Our wills are ours only to give away. The human heart is torn between a sense of emptiness and a need of being filled, like the water pots of Cana. The emptiness comes from the fact that we are human. The power of filling belongs only to Him Who ordered the water pots filled. Lest any heart should fail in being filled. Mary's last valedictory is: "Whatsoever He shall say to you, that do ye." The heart has a need of emptying and a need of being filled. The power of emptying is human — emptying in the love of others — the power of filling belongs only to God. Hence all perfect love must end on the note: "Not my will, but Thine be done, O Lord."

World Peace

LET THE ENEMY COME as so many armored and panoplied Goliaths, thinking that steel must always be met by steel alone, and we shall, like other Davids, go out to meet them unto victory, clothed in the power of Him Who gave to the evil of this earth its one mortal wound — an open tomb, a gaping sepulcher, an empty grave.

Whence shall come our hope for peace? It will not come from the common man unpurified by faith; for once in power, he will cease to be the common man, the proletarian, and will become the uncommon man, the bureaucrat.

Rather we must trust in the common man made uncommon by the Power of Him Who dared to say to the first of all totalitarian Caesars of Christian history: "Thou shouldst not have any power...unless it were given thee from above" (John 19:11).

Scars of War

AS A SOLDIER MAY RETURN FROM WAR wearing the ribbons of victory, so Jesus rises from the dead wearing the scars of battle against sin! Everywhere in the Easter scenes, we meet a Great Soldier with His Scars! Mary Magdalene, who had anointed His Feet for His burial just a few days before and then once again knelt at His Feet on Calvary's hill, now on Easter morn recognizes Him to be not the gardener but the Risen Savior, as clinging to His Feet she sees there the livid red memories of riven steel.

As the ten Apostles and their companions gathered around the evening lamp in conversation with the travelers of Emmaus, suddenly, silently, without shadow, sound, without the lifting of a bolt or the stirring of the latch, Jesus appears in the midst of them, saying: "Peace be upon you: it is Myself, do not be afraid." Cowering in terror, He reassures them, saying: "Look at My Hands and My Feet to be assured that it is Myself; touch Me and look." And as He spoke thus, He showed them His Hands and His Feet (Luke 24:39-40). Hands that had lifted up blind eyes to the sight of God's sunshine, Feet that climbed the mountain's stairs to a midnight Holy of Holies to pray — but now Hands and Feet that show like luminous stars!

Later on, Thomas, the individualist, who was not with the other Apostles when the Savior appeared — missing spiritual opportunities may cause doubt — when he was told by the Disciples: "We have seen the Lord," answered: "Until I have seen the mark of the nails and put my hand into His Side, you will never make me *believe*" (John 20:25).

Close Your Eyes

YOU HAVE FIVE SENSES which put you in touch with the material and sensate passing world about you. But did you ever notice that when you wish to do deep thinking you shut your eyes, close the doors of the ear to the rattles of earth, for the more you shut out the things of earth, the more the Spirit of God speaks within you. You will learn more truth from the Spirit than from books, as the Apostles on Pentecost learned more about the Life of Christ than they did from three years of living with Him in an earthly way.

The Power of Our Blessed Lord while on earth was sometimes exercised through immediate personal contact, such as when He laid His Fingers on the eyes of the blind man. At other times He cured at a distance, as He did the servant of the centurion.

Moments of Great Catastrophe Are Often the Eves of Great Spiritual Renaissance

IT WAS NOT WHEN THE APOSTLES SAW CHRIST in the transient glory of Transfiguration but in the ignominy of a tortured man on the Cross that they were closest to their victory. Our Divine Lord Himself, speaking of wars, rumors of wars, earthquakes and distress of nations, makes the forecast of these calamities the very motive of hope: "But when these things begin to come to pass, look up and lift your heads because your redemption is at hand" (Luke 21:28).

The reason moments of catastrophe may be the eves of spiritual victory is because it is in those moments of defeat that man's pride is most humbled and his soul thus prepared for the help of God. Israel received her greatest prophets in the hour when all hope seemed gone. The prodigal son was closest to his greatest joy when his substance had been wasted. It is only when Peter had labored all the night and taken nothing that he was given the miraculous draught of fishes. And in the spiritual life "the dark night of the soul," the purification of the senses by mortification, is the prelude to the rapturous joys of the Spirit. I believe we are now in such an age, of which Isaiah spoke: "I will give thee the treasure of darkness" (Isaiah 45:3). Darkness may be creative, for it is there that God plants his seeds to grow and his bulbs to flower. It is at night that the sheep which are scattered are gathered into the unity of the sheepfold, when the children come home to their mother and the soul back again to God. Daylight deceives us, but as we awake at night, we get a new sense of values; darkness seems to tell the awful truth. As the psalmist put it: "Day to day uttereth speech and night to night showeth knowledge" (Psalm 18:3). Night has its wonders, as well as day; darkness is not final, except to those who are without God.

When We Suffer

When we suffer, we do not want one
Who stands over us like a physician,
Who touches us as tongs touch hot coals,
Who washes in antiseptic after contact,
And who parrots: "Keep your chin up."

We want One Who left footprints
In the dark forest — so we can follow.
A Surgeon Who, before He cuts,
Says: "I had the same — see My Scars!"
Someone Who stumbled to a Throne
And walked not unfallen to the Hill.

We want One Who, as we question:
"Does God know what it is to suffer?"
Can point to riven Side and open Heart,
Saying: "Wouldst thou not be nobler than I
If thou couldst suffer for Love,
And I could not?"

Yes! Christ is Judge. But until that
Great Assize, when heaven's ledgers are brought
    forth,
He says: "I sentence you to death —
But I shall pay the penalty
And let you free."

Is Pain a Waste?

THERE IS IN EACH OF US a shadow-self and a real-self. The shadow-self seeks only its own will and pleasure. The more we keep the sun behind us, the greater the length of the shadow.

Every pain patiently borne, every blow to self, shapes the real eternal self. It was the Crucifixion of Our Lord that prepared the way for His Resurrection and Glory.

If you live for Christ, not the slightest moment of your life goes to waste. Does not a mother often set aside suitable gifts or even a dowry for her daughter's wedding before love has ever come into her life? Our Lord is weaving your heavenly robes for the heavenly nuptials, though you know it not, in moments that seem so loveless.

You cannot see entirely God's Plan for you. The uncharted ocean is before you, as you toss in the narrow cabin of your suffering; but the Divine Pilot is bringing you to port.

When you receive Communion, you are united to the Life of Christ. He lives in you and you live in Him;

but you are also incorporated in his *Death*. St. Paul says that as often as we receive the Eucharist, we announce the Death of the Lord until He comes.

Think of the multitudes that thronged about Our Lord when He was on earth, eager to be healed or taught or fed or thrilled by a miracle. It sometimes wounded the Sacred Heart, for He said: "You followed Me because you did eat and were filled." What a joy it was for Him to find in the crowd one or two who followed Him just because they loved Him and not because they wanted something from Him. When the prodigal son left home, he said, "Give me." He wanted something. When he returned home a much wiser but sadder youth, he said, "Make me." God, too, has His "golddiggers" — those who want more gold mixed with the alloy of earth. Few there are who offer Him the gold of their life, in order that He might put it through the crucible of suffering and burn out the alloy of sin and imperfection.

When the Doors Are Locked

EASTER SUNDAY EVENING the Apostles gathered in the upper room because of fear of the people who might have been provoked to violence because of the stories circulating about the Resurrection of Christ. While assembled there out of fear, Jesus came and stood in the midst of them and said: "Peace be unto you" (John 20:19). How He came, they knew not. They only knew that the chamber was securely locked against intrusion or surprise; no bolt was withdrawn, no door was open, no breach was made in the wall, there was no visible movement from without or within or from point to point. One moment they were alone and the next moment they looked and beheld a form, a visible body and face, a solid human frame was before them, as if created out of the atmosphere. He, the Risen Christ, spoke those words that follow every victorious war: "Peace be unto you."

In the heart of apparent failure, in the midst of darkest human fear, doors locked against enemies,

God's Power is most clearly revealed. When the world's predicament is most desperate, there is a breaking in of a new factor from the outside which completely changes the situation. When chaos and fear and the powers of darkness seem invincible, the Purpose of God moves on.

As there was a Divine invasion in Bethlehem, so too, there is now a Divine invasion after Calvary. As the Jews of old were saved from bondage at the Red Sea, by the Hand of the Lord dividing the waters for them, the same waters swallowing up their pursuers, so too now when men huddle together in fear, the Power of God becomes manifest. The Kingdom of God does not grow *out* of history, but manifests itself *through* history, as the Divine intrudes into the order of space and time.

The Church and Persecution

BE NOT CAST DOWN because the persecutors of religion, having laid the Church, like its Founder, in the tomb, utter the boast: "Behold the place where we laid it." The law of progress of the Church is the reverse of the law of progress of the world. We are most progressive when we are most hated.

Whence shall come our hope for the Church? It will not come from the world, for if the world loved the Church, the Church would be no salvation to the world. If it were not hated, it would be weak. It is only because the fires of its Truth are blinding evil eyes and convicting them of sin and judgment, that the world vainly tried to put them out. And though the world is tearing up all the photographs and blueprints of a society and a family based on the moral law of God, be not disheartened. The Church has kept the negatives.

Francis Thompson compared the Church to the lily, depicting first its defeat, then its resurrection, in these magnificent lines:

> "O Lily of the King! low lies thy silver
> wing,

And long has been the hour of thine
      unqueening;
And thy scent of Paradise on the night
      wind spills its sighs,
Nor any take the secrets of its meaning.
O Lily of the King! I speak a heavy thing,
O patience, most sorrowful of daughters!
Lo, the hour is at hand for the troubling of
      the land,
And red shall be the breaking of the
      waters.
Sit fast upon thy stalk, when the blast shall
      with thee talk,
With the mercies of the King for thine
      awning;
And the just understand that thine hour is
      at hand,
Thine hour at hand with power in the
      dawning.
When the nations lie in blood, and their
      kings a broken brood,
Look up, O most sorrowful of daughters!
Lift up thy head and hark what sounds are
      in the dark,
For His Feet are coming to thee on the
      water!"

"LILIUM REGIS"

No Shadow without Light

IF NATURE WERE INDIFFERENT to infractions of its laws, if health did not decline with the refusal to eat, if blindness did not follow the plucking out of an eye, if one gathered figs of thistles and if water ran uphill, it would be difficult to believe that Supreme Intelligence had imposed order and law on the visible universe in which we live.

If the moral order were indifferent to our infractions, if the breakdown of the nations did not follow the collapse of family life, if the affirmation that man is an animal did not make men act like animals, if the denial that God is the Author of Law did not produce a lawless and therefore a warring world, it would be difficult to believe that God made a moral universe in which men reaped what they sowed and where the wages of sin are death.

At no time in modern history has it been easier to believe in God than now. It used to be that evil was considered a stumbling block to a belief in the Goodness of God, but today men are coming to a belief in the Goodness of God because of evil. They admit that evil today has taken on such proportions that it can be explained only by the infraction of a universal moral law that must have come from God. In a word, the modern man is coming to God by way of the devil.

Such is the lesson of this Resurrection Day: We come to the glory of Easter Sunday through the evil of a Good Friday, to a halo of dazzling light through the ignominy of a crown of thorns, to the dawn of a new day through the darkness of a high noon.

Calvary is only a momentary scandal. Goodness in the face of evil must suffer, for when love meets sin it will be crucified. A God Who bears His Sacred Heart upon His sleeve, as Our Lord did in the Incarnation, must be prepared to have crows peck at it. But at the same time, Goodness can use that suffering as the condition of overcoming evil! It can take anger and wrath and hate and say "Forgive." It can take life and offer it for another. Evil may have its hour, but God will have His day.

Where Persecution Reigns

WE ARE LIVING IN A PERIOD OF HISTORY like unto that of the Roman Empire when Julian the Apostate sat upon the throne of the Caesars. The persecution of Christ, which he initiated, was not like the earlier persecutions, which were prompted by the release of a barbaric instinct, but rather was due to the perversion and the loss of faith in Christ. Like his successors in the modern world, Julian persecuted because he had lost his faith — and since his conscience would not let him alone, he would not let the Church alone.

He made a tour of the Roman Empire to investigate the success of his persecutions. He came to the ancient city of Antioch where, disguising himself, he entered into the inns, taverns and public markets, better to learn the fruits of his hate. On one occasion, watching thousands of people crowd into a temple dedicated to Mithra, he was recognized by an old Christian friend whose name was Agathon. Pointing to the crowd and to the apparent success of the pagan cult, he sneered this question to his friend: "Agathon, what ever happened to that carpenter of Galilee — does he have any jobs these days?" Agathon answered: "He is building a coffin now for the Roman Empire — and for you."

Six months later Julian thrust a dagger into his own heart. Throwing it toward the heavens against which he had rebelled, as his own unredemptive blood fell back upon him, he uttered his last and most famous line: "O Galilean, Thou hast conquered." He always does!

Despair of Disciples

EASTER AFTERNOON, when Our Blessed Lord becomes the fellow traveler of His Disciples on the way to Emmaus, He finds them also downcast with despair because they had hopes that it was He who would have redeemed Israel, but now it is three days since He is dead.

Seven days later Thomas the Apostle, still refusing to believe the good news, says that he will not *believe* until he can put his fingers into His Hands and his hand into His Side. In that moment Our Lord appears: "Put in thy finger hither and see My Hands and bring hither thy hand and put it into My Side and be not faithless, but *believe*." Apparently the one thing that the Apostles and lovers of Our Blessed Lord were not expecting was His Resurrection from the dead and when He appeared in their midst, He said, to rebuke their fears, "Why are you troubled and why do doubts arise in your hearts?"

Well indeed may Our Lord say the same to us: "Why are you troubled in heart, despairing and cast down? Are you seeking security, rather than the happiness of the Resurrection?" Too often, we are like those who, taking an ocean journey, are more concerned with the life belts than with the cabin; or, traveling by air, are more interested with the parachute than the beauty of God's sky; or, traveling the highway, are less happy about the ride than looking for first-aid stations. Rather with St. Paul should we say: "If Christ is not risen, then we are all men most miserable." Shall we believe that God reserves all the mourning for His sons and all the joys for His enemies. Are we condemned to hang our harps upon the willows and sing nothing but doleful dirges, while the children of Satan are to laugh with gladness of heart?

No, rather we have received not the spirit of bondage to fear but the spirit of adoption, whereby we cry out: "Father!" Fear not! Realize that He Who went into that grave is Truth Itself and Truth crushed to earth will rise again. Dostoevsky tells us the story of two men looking at a painting by Holbein, *The Taking of Christ from the Cross*. One said: "I like looking at that picture." The other said: "Some people's faith has been ruined by that picture." And right he was! That picture would ruin the faith of a materialist, an atheist, a Communist, and all who believe that there is nothing after this life. If there is no Resurrection, but

Christ is dead, one cannot believe either in the Goodness of God or the goodness of man. But if He Who took the worst the world had to offer and conquered it, then evil shall never be victorious again.

The Cup

"Am I not to drink that Cup which My
Father Himself has appointed for me?"

JOHN 18:11

This question was asked of Peter at the moment
when Peter took his sword from its sheath, gave a
wild swing and hacked off the ear of the servant of a
high priest. Peter, who now displays so much military
valor, had just a few hours before that succumbed to
the question of a girl in the court of Caiphas and
swore and cursed that he knew not "the Man." In this
act of Peter and in the words of Our Lord is the
distinction between military valor and Christian fortitude. Military valor is boisterous and is better for its
sudden onset than a deliberate trial, but Christian
fortitude depends on the strength of faith and lies in
the meek subjection to God, even in the midst of
torments.

The particular analogy which Our Blessed Lord
used was that of a Cup, which in Scripture often refers
to sorrow and tribulation.

Notice that Our Blessed Lord did not say "the Cup which Caiphas gave Me," or "Pilate gave," or "Judas gave," or His own people, or even the sins of the world. He said it was the "Father Who gave Me the Cup." Should he not drink it? Human instruments were merely the gloves which touched the Cup, but the Hand inside of the glove was the Providential Hand of the Father.

Magdalene in the Garden

THE SUPREME INSTANCE OF ALL HISTORY that the voice of the people is not necessarily the Voice of God was the moment when a mob passed beneath a Cross, flinging at the helpless figure there upon it the blistering sneer of the ages: "He trusted in God; let him now deliver *him*" (Matthew 27:43).

Two days later, early in the morning, a converted sinner is found walking in a cemetery — she whose heart had been captured by Him without, as other men had done, laying it waste. She was in search of a tomb and a dead body which she hoped she might anoint with spices.

The idea of the Resurrection did not seem to enter her mind — she who herself had risen from a tomb sealed by the seven devils of sin. Finding the tomb empty, she broke again into a fountain of tears. No one who weeps ever looks upward. With her eyes cast down as the brightness of the early sunrise swept over the dew-covered grass, she vaguely perceived someone near her, who asked: "Woman, why weepest thou?" (John 20:15).

Mary, thinking it might have been the gardener, said: "Because they have taken away My Lord and I do not know where they have laid Him."

The figure before her spoke only one word, one name, and in a tone so sweet and ineffably tender that it could be the only unforgettable voice of the world — and that one word was "Mary."

No one could ever say "Mary" as He said it. In that moment she knew Him. Dropping into the Aramaic of her mother's speech, she answered but one word: *"Rabboni!* (Master!)." And she fell at His Feet — she was always there, anointing them at a supper, standing before them at a Cross and now kneeling before Him in the Glory of an Easter morn.

The After-Death Friends

WHEN OUR LORD SURRENDERED HIS SPIRIT to the Heavenly Father on Good Friday and was cold like all dead men, friends who had shut themselves up in their houses and anonymous admirers who hid their light under a bushel now began to appear. They were not with Him in His agony when He needed them, but they were with Him in His death, as weavers of wreaths, as weepers of glittering tears and as eulogists of the dead. One of these friends was Joseph of Arimathea who, secretly loving the Savior, was yet not bold enough to declare it while He was alive. He would now diminish his remorse by providing a tomb for the executed friend. This rich councillor boldly goes to Pilate and asks to have the Body of Jesus. Joseph's purpose was to save Our Blessed Lord from a dishonorable burial, i.e., from being cast into a dump, where criminals were thrown and sometimes burned.

Pilate was surprised that Our Lord was already dead and sent for the centurion to give an official verdict concerning His Death. After Pilate heard the report of the centurion, he granted the request of Joseph of Arimathea. Joseph then goes back to Calvary, takes Our Lord down from the Cross, wraps Him in a winding sheet which he had bought, and they lay Him in a tomb cut out of a rock. A stranger's tomb alone was fitting for Him Who is a stranger to Death.

Atlas and Christ

OPPOSITE ST. PATRICK'S CATHEDRAL in New York is a giant statue of Atlas, bending and groaning and grunting under the weight of the world. That is modern man! "The world is too much with him, late and soon." The world is too heavy for him and man is breaking under it, trying like a silly child to carry it alone, without any help or grace or faith from God.

The other image I see is that of the God-Man on Good Friday, carrying a Cross, taking upon Himself the burden of others and proving that sacrifice for sin, selflessness and love of God and neighbor alone can remake the world.

No one will get out of this world without carrying some burden. Atlas will never get out from under that world; the Man Who carried the Cross will get out from under it, for it leads to Resurrection and a crown in Life Eternal. This is the choice before us: either try to revolutionize the world and break under it or revolutionize ourselves and remake the world.

Cross Asks Questions, Easter Answers Them

THE CROSS HAD ASKED THE QUESTIONS; the Resurrection had answered them. The Cross had asked the question: "How far can Power go in the world?" The Resurrection answered: "Power ends in its own destruction, for those who slew the foe lost the day."

The Cross had asked: "Why does God permit evil and sin to nail Justice to a tree?" The Resurrection answered: "That sin, having done its worst, might exhaust itself and thus be overcome by Love that is stronger than either sin or death."

Thus there emerges the Easter lesson that the power of evil and the chaos of any one moment can be defied and conquered, for the basis of our hope is not in any construct of human power but in the Power of God, who has given to the evil of this earth its one mortal wound — an open tomb, a gaping sepulcher, an empty grave.

If the story of Christ ended with that cry of abandonment on the Cross, then what hope have we that bruised Goodness and crucified Justice will ever rise triumphant over the massed wickedness of men?

If He Who died to give us the glorious liberty of the children of God could not break the chains of death, then what hope is there that the enslaved peoples of the world will ever rise from the slavery of their graves to a freedom where a man can call his soul his own?

Pilate Condemns

"DID YOU KNOW THAT I WAS SILENT seven times at My trial? I spoke as a Shepherd; I was silent as a sheep. I spoke as Teacher; I was silent as the Lamb. My silence disturbed Pilate, but what could I say? I was guilty. I was carrying your sins. I could not make excuses."

The Two Trees

⤳

IN GENESIS 2:9 we read of "the tree of the knowledge of good and evil." In Acts 5:30 we are told "the God of our fathers raised up Jesus, Who you slew and hanged on a *tree*." And again in 1 Peter 2:24 "who bore our sins on the tree." The fact that the Cross is spoken of as a tree has a very deep meaning and harkens back to the Garden of Eden.

The first tree was planned by God (Genesis 2:9): the tree of the knowledge of good and evil. The second tree was planned not by God but by man on the hill of Calvary.

Man was forbidden to draw near the first tree, but is invited to come to the second, which is the Cross. Because of the first tree, man is driven out of Paradise; because of the second tree, man is permitted to re-enter.

Both trees were planted in a garden: "Now in the place where He was crucified, there was a garden" (John 19:41).

As the tree of the knowledge of good and evil was in the "midst" of the garden (Genesis 2:9), so Our Lord was crucified in the midst of good and evil.

In Exodus 15:23-25 we have the story of Israel at the commencement of the wilderness journey toward Marah, whose waters they could not drink because they were bitter, and Moses cried to the Lord. The Lord showed him a tree, which he cast into the waters and they were made sweet. It was Our Blessed Lord Who sweetened the bitter waters of life by His Death for us.

Evil Will Never Conquer

JESUS OF THE SCARS assured us that evil will never have an ultimate victory. The worst thing that evil can do is not to bomb cities but to kill Goodness itself. But being defeated in its mightiest moment, when evil used its strongest arms by His Resurrection from the dead, we may be sure that it will never be victorious again. Well, indeed, may the nail-torn Christ say: "I have overcome the world."

Jesus of the Scars knows what death is, for He is the only One Who ever came to this world to die. Everyone else comes to live. Death was a stumbling block to Socrates; it interrupted the teaching of Buddha. But to Christ it was the goal of His Life, the gold that He was seeking. Breaking those bonds of the grave, by His Resurrection, He has taught us to say: "O Death, where is thy victory? O Grave, where is thy sting?" No longer can men say there are no tears in the eyes of the Eternal, no pain in the heart of God. Take then your Christ with lily-white Hands, with uncrimsoned robes and unpierced Brows, and Eyes undimmed by sorrow! Take Him from our midst! He is too soft for these hard days!

Scarred men come for healing only to scarred hands! Only a Risen Jesus with Scars can understand our hearts. This is not an age of wars but an age of scars! We all have scars! *Everybody!* Scars on bodies — the wounds of war; scars on souls — the wounds of godlessness. Scars of hate, fear, anxiety, melancholy, bitterness! Either scars fighting against Thee or scars fighting with Thee! Scars born of the offensive against Love; Scars born of the defense of Love!

The Victim of Love

You think you swept all love away
As many autumns shook the years like leaves
'Til now all your loves
Were as a barter and exchange:
The sweet reciprocal: "I love you, you love Me."

But two deeper loves are left you still:
One to be used in time;
The other, in eternity.

The first, the seeming unreciprocated love
Wherein you love Him Who left a wound,
Though He, in turn, is silent.
But you, like Job, cry out:
"I will love Him though He slay me.

To love Him because we *feel* His Love
Is to be repaid a thousandfold.
But to love through a dumb and unechoing love
Is to be one with Him
Who, in the body-shuddering solitude of the Cross,
Felt so unloved by man.

This armless, lipless love,
Which seems so cold,
Is but the novitiate to that other Love,
Which waits thee in eternity,
Wherein you shall be dumb and speechless
With ecstasies of Jesu, *voluptas cordium.*

Complain

God does not frown on your complaint.
Did not His Mother in the Temple ask:
"Son! Why hast Thou done so to us?"
And did not Christ on the Cross complain:
"My God! Why hast Thou abandoned Me?"
If the Son asked the Father
And the Mother the Son: "Why?"
Why should not you?

But let your wails be to God
And not to man,
Asking not: "Why does God do this to me?"
But, "Why, O God, does Thou treat me so?"
Talk not *about* God, as Satan did to Eve:
"Why did God command you?"
But talk *to* God, as Christ to His Father.

And at the end of your sweet complaining prayer
You will say: "Father, into Thy Hands I commend my
spirit."
You will not so much ask to be taken down,

As the thief on the left,
But to be taken up, as the thief
Who heard: "This Day, Paradise."

They who complain to others never see God's
    purposes
They who complain to God find that
Their Passion, like Christ's, turns into compassion.

Why Should Not I Be Immune from a Cross?

❦

"WHY SHOULD NOT I BE IMMUNE from suffering?" This was the question that was asked in the very first century, when joining the Church very often meant martyrdom. St. Peter had to answer that particular difficulty, saying:

> "Do not be surprised, Beloved, that this fiery ordeal should have befallen you, to test your quality. There is nothing strange in what is happening to you. Rather, rejoice when you share in some measure the sufferings of Christ; so joy will be yours, and triumph, when His Glory is revealed."
>
> 2 PETER 4:12-13

Peter bids the converts from paganism not to think that suffering was strange or alien to the Christian nature. They could be somewhat excused for this point of view for they had no background of a long line of Christian ancestors, as we do. Peter, however, explains to them that the suffering is a smelting process likened to that of the ancient goldsmith who refined crude gold ore in his crucible, burning away the dross in intense heat to recover the pure gold. Like the goldsmith, God keeps us in the smelting furnace until He can see the reflection of the Face of the Lord Jesus in our lives. He is not so much interested in the work we do, but rather in how much we resemble His Son. Holy people are to rejoice in the fact that they are coparticipants in the sufferings of Christ.

Guarding a Tomb

THE NEWS HAD SPREAD that Our Blessed Lord had been given an honorable burial by Joseph, the rich man. Like a bolt out of the blue, the Pharisees run to Pilate to protest against the delivery of the Body to Joseph. As they claimed His Life, so they would claim His Death. Once in Pilate's presence, they said: "Sir, we have recalled it to memory that this deceiver, while he yet lied, said, 'I am to rise again after three days!' Give orders, then, that this tomb shall be securely guarded until the third day or perhaps his Disciples will come and steal him away. If they should then say to the people, 'He has risen from the dead,' this last deceit will be more dangerous than the old" (Matthew 27:63-65).

Pilate was angry and retorted: "You have guards. Away with you. Make it secure as you best know how." With the double guard of the Romans and the Pharisees, Scripture now tells, "They went and made the tomb secure, putting a seal on the stone and setting a guard over it."

They insured against fraud in two ways. First of all, the stone which they placed there was, in the language of the Gospels, "exceedingly great," and second, it was sealed. This would prevent anyone from touching the body.

In the history of the world there was never a more ridiculous spectacle than that of a hundred soldiers stationed to keep an eye on a corpse. No other grave on the face of the earth was ever watched, because the dead man said that He would rise in three days. But here guards are set, lest the dead walk, the silent speak and the pierced heart quicken to the throb of life. They say He is dead; they know He is dead; they will tell you that He will not rise again; *but still they watch.* They called Our Lord a deceiver. Will He still deceive? Has He deceived them into believing that He Who lost the battle will really win the war?

They Call Christ a deceiver! That He is! Only a deceiver like Christ can please us, for we have already been deceived. The world is our first deceiver! It promised us peace and gave us war; it promised us enduring love and gave us age and satiety!

Come then, O Christ, our other deceiver, Thou dost seem so stern, so hard, for Thou art, "purpureal robed and cypress crowned." Thou does seem to crucify our flesh and our eros. At first glance, we shrink from Thee, saying: "Must all Thy fields be dunged with rotten death?" But oh! what sweet deceit, for as we come to know Thee, we find in Thee that love we sought for when the world worked on us its first deceit!

Heavenly traitor! that seemed so dead and yet are the Risen Life! Deceive us with Thy Scars — that our weak souls break free and throw us back to Thee!

The Future Easter

THE WORLD MAY BE IN THE THROES of a new birth, when the Christian message shall pass from the Western to the Eastern world. Within a short time the Mystical Christ, Who has been crucified, will take His bleeding Hands to the Japanese, who will lay their lotus flower upon them to change the wounds of hate into the scars of love. To the Chinese, He will bring His bruised and torn Body, and the weak and lame and blind, the hungry and the famished will bring their healing hands and cover up from sight those imprints of a night forever past. To the people of India, He will show His open wounded Side, and they who sought their peace in a nirvana of unconsciousness will be drowned at last in the Sacred Heart in a love that is a healing of the soul.

Finally, He Who went into darkness through a crown of thorns will turn to Africa and the people of the midnight Madonnas and they shall pluck out His thorns and crown Him with blossoms and with flowers as white as their souls, as perfumed as their faith.

The News Has Not Yet Leaked Out

IF THE BASIS OF CHRISTIANITY were anything else than a God Who came from a tomb, then we would be without hope. If He were a worldly success, then we would have to imitate Him in worldliness. If He were a failure and never rose from defeat, then we would be vindictive and hate the Jews, the Romans and the Greeks, who symbolized the world that crucified Him. If He were only a man, He would be forgotten, as all men are. If He wrote a book, we would all have to be professors, but since He came into this world to bring victory out of defeat, then the more hopeless the situation, the more certainly does the Divine Power operate.

How long this conflict between good and evil will last we do not know; how long we will walk down the road bemoaning persecutions and Crucifixions before He makes His Presence known to us we do not know; how long we will seek the living among the dead, as did Magdalene, we know not; how long we will crouch in fear behind closed doors before the Light of

the world breaks through with "Peace be unto you,"
we do not know. There is only one thing we do know
and that is that we have already won — only the news
has not yet leaked out!

Enlarging Our Power To Be Joyful

OUR BLESSED LORD DOES NOT SPEAK OF SORROW being exchanged for joy but of its being transmitted so that the grief becomes a joy. Our present groanings are creating within us a larger capacity for joy hereafter. St. Paul said:

"This light and momentary affliction brings with it a reward multiplied every way, loading us with everlasting glory; if only we will fix our eyes on what is unseen, not on what we can see" (2 Corinthians 4:17-18).

But how fearful is the contrast in the case of unbelievers, as Our Lord said:

"Woe upon you who laugh now; you shall mourn and weep" (Luke 6:25).

Our Blessed Lord, in order to portray this changing of cross into glory and suffering into joy, compares life to a mother bringing a child into the world. The very force of the figure used intimates the necessity of suffering, the severity of it, its brief duration and the fact that it is antecedent and productive of joy. The labor pangs of mortification are the precursors of resurrection and joy. To those who have faith, all pangs are birth pangs.

Notice how sorrow springs from the same root as gladness. The two do not clash against each other, but they blend into one another. Our purest and noblest joys are transformed sorrows. The sorrow of a contrite heart becomes the gladness of pardoned children. Every stroke of the ploughshare and every dark winter's day are represented in the broad acres waving with golden wheat. In suffering, Christ takes you into His Hands as a poor, dull block of marble, but with His chisel He shapes His Purpose in you.

Divine Healer

Only He Who made your wound can heal it.
The Love that tightened your bow strings
Did so, not in hurt but in love of music.

Do not all lovers ask in doubt: "Do you love me?"
Ask that of the Tremendous Lover
And each Scar will seem a kiss!

God is not "way up there."
He is taking another body — your own
To carry on the world's redemption.

Too few offer Him a human nature
Like Mary at the Angel's call —
So He conscripts you, drafts you,
Inducts you into His Army.

Complain that your shoulders
ache beneath your pack —
But see His own smarting
under a Cross beam.

Complaint to God is dialogue
And dialogue is prayer,
Not the ready-made, packaged, memorized
Lip service of the book and candle,
But the encounter and the union
That only lovers know!

Transmute Your Pain

DO NOT THINK that you have to be in personal contact with a sinful world in order to do it good. The most powerful influences are the invisible ones. You can save a sinner in India, give courage to a leper in Africa, console the bereaved in Bosnia by offering your cross. You can be like the clouds that gather up moisture from one body of water and then transport it over mountain heights, letting it fall as gentle dew on distant parched lands.

When a trial or difficulty, a sorrow or cross comes into your life, remember that you are like a child practicing a new lesson. As the child in the first grade is on his way to being a great musician, a linguist, a scientist, so you, under the guidance of the Divine Teacher, are on the way to being a saint, for then you shall be flooded with the joy that no one can take from you.

Do not publicize your sufferings or even your patience in suffering. It is only the God-unblessed projects that seek newspaper publicity. There is more wisdom, more power and promise of blessing in the instructions of Our Blessed Lord: "Say nothing to any-one..."

The tragedy of any life is not what happens, it is rather how we react to what happens. Those who do not profit from the things that happen to them generally carry around with them through life open infectious wounds. But those who know that God is working out a Plan in them that one day will be revealed learn from the incidents of life, as St. Paul suggested:

> "...we are confident even over our afflictions, knowing well that affliction gives rise to endurance, and endurance gives proof of our faith, and a proved faith gives ground for hope. Nor does this hope delude us; the love of God has been poured out in our hearts by the Holy Spirit."
>
> ROMANS 5:3-6

Captains of Wars

THERE ARE TWO KINDS OF UNBELIEF: those who say something is not true *because* they *wish* it were not true and those who say something is not true because they wish that it was. This latter kind is curable. After eight days of the gloom that comes from doubt, the Savior appears to the doubter, Thomas, and says: "Let me have thy finger; see, here are My Hands. Let me have thy hand; put it into My Side. Cease thy doubting and believe" (John 20:27). Thomas casts himself at His Feet, saying: "My Lord and my God" (John 20:28).

"O Captain of the wars!

Why wear ye these Scars?"

First, to prove the law of Christian life that no one shall be crowned unless he has struggled; that no crowns of merit rest suspended on those who do not fight; that unless there is a Good Friday in our lives there will never be an Easter Sunday; that no one ever rises to a higher life without death to a lower one; that God hates peace in those who are destined for war.

Second, to prove His Love. True love seeks not its own good, but the good of the other. As human love relieves the physical pains of others, so Divine Love relieves the moral evils of others. True love is proven not by words but by offering something to the one loved and the greatest offering one can give is not what one *has* but one's very life. Every Scar tells the story: "Greater love than this no man hath."

Third, to solicit our love, He rose, not with wounds for those would betoken a weakness after battle but with Scars, glorious medals of victory on Hands and Feet and Side. As a little child may say to a wounded or scarred soldier: "How did that happen?" so Our Lord shows us His Scars, that by our childish questioning, He might tell us:"I did this all for you!"

Reluctance Changed to Joy

HE WHO HAS LONG BEEN UNDER THE ROD OF GOD
becomes God's possession. The consolation Our Lord
gives is not always to cool our fevered brow or heal
our broken limb but to give us a vision of His purpos-
es, so that we hasten to use every pain to save souls,
to repair our own sins and those of others.

See how Simon of Cyrene was consoled. He who
halved the Cross of Our Lord was from Africa. Was he
a Negro? We do not know for certain. In the ACTS,
there is a Simon, the Black Man, mentioned. In any
case, Africa was the first country to share the Cross of
Christ. A poem by Countee Cullen tells the story of
unwillingness turned to joy:

"At first I said, 'I will not bear
His Cross upon my back;
He only seeks to place it there
Because my skin is black.'
But He was dying for a dream,
And He was very meek;
And in His Eyes there shone a gleam
Men journey far to seek.

It was Himself my pity brought,
I did for Christ alone
What all of Rome could not have wrought
With bruise, or lash or stone."

Oh! that we could die in pairs: husband and wife, lover and beloved, widow and only son, friend and friend. But we die singly that at death we might, by our free choice, be paired with Christ, as the thief on the right: "This day, thou shalt be with Me in Paradise."

The Complexity of Man

WHATEVER MAN IS, he is not what he ought to be. He has all of the machinery, but the mainspring is broken. He is like a fish on top of the Empire State Building.

Modern psychology which explains the tension between the lower and the higher self, between man and his environment, is but a psychological description of the fall of man. Furthermore, it explains why all men are alike in their bias or tendency toward evil. "In Adam all die."

HOW THE DEVIL TEMPTS

He tempts by a dialogue which is pious and religious. He does not say: "I am an atheistic monster and I'm going to destroy your innocence and your loyalty." He merely begins by saying: "Let's have a little panel show today, children. We are going to talk about God." He did not deny God; he assumed God. The devil believes in God.

In the desert when Our Lord was tempted, he did not say to Our Lord: "You are a fool to obey your

Heavenly Father." *He quoted Sacred Scripture.* He always acts in *disguise.* All temptations begin in sugar form.

As Mephistopheles in *Faust* says, "The people never know the devil is there, even though he has them by the throat."

The devil appears as the representative of good. No one does evil for the mere sake of evil. Evil is done for the seeming good that is in it. The devil knows that we are not so depraved that we want to do evil.

Sanctity

Sanctity, then, is not giving up the world. It is exchanging the world. It is a continuation of that sublime transaction of the Incarnation in which Christ said to man: "You give Me your humanity, I will give you My Divinity. You give Me your time, I will give you My Eternity. You give Me your bonds, I will give you My Omnipotence. You give Me your slavery, I will give you My Freedom. You give Me your death, I will give you My Life. You give Me your nothingness, I will give you My All." And the consoling thought throughout this whole transforming process is that it does not require much time to make us saints; it requires only much love.

Cannot Make Best of Two Worlds

"FEAR YE NOT THEM THAT KILL THE BODY...but rather fear him that can destroy both soul and body in hell." Calvary is wrapped up in these words of our Blessed Lord, for therein is revealed the supreme struggle of every life — the struggle to preserve our spiritual freedom. We cannot serve both God and Mammon; we cannot save our life both for time and eternity; we cannot feast both here and hereafter; we cannot make the best of two worlds; either we will have the fast on earth and the feast in heaven or we will have the feast here and the fast in eternity.

Without Me...Nothing

LIGHT IS NOT IN THE EYE, but the eyes see because of it; food is not in the stomach, but it is thanks to food that the body lives; sound is not in the ear, but it is thanks to harmony that the ear hears. In the spiritual order it is the same: what air is to the lungs, prayer is to the soul. As Our Lord said, "Without Me, you can do nothing." He did not mean that we could do nothing in the natural order without Him, but He meant that we could do nothing in the spiritual order without His grace.

Additional Titles Published by Resurrection Press, a Catholic Book Publishing Imprint

A Rachel Rosary Larry Kupferman	$4.50
Blessings All Around Dolores Leckey	$8.95
Catholic Is Wonderful Mitch Finley	$4.95
Come, Celebrate Jesus! Francis X. Gaeta	$4.95
From Holy Hour to Happy Hour Francis X. Gaeta	$7.95
Healing through the Mass Robert DeGrandis, SSJ	$9.95
The Healing Rosary Mike D.	$5.95
Healing Your Grief Ruthann Williams, OP	$7.95
Healthy and Holy Under Stress Muto, VanKaam	$3.95
Heart Peace Adolfo Quezada	$9.95
Life, Love and Laughter Jim Vlaun	$7.95
Living Each Day by the Power of Faith Barbara Ryan	$8.95
The Joy of Being a Catechist Gloria Durka	$4.95
The Joy of Being a Eucharistic Minister Mitch Finley	$5.95
The Joy of Preaching Rod Damico	$6.95
The Joy of Ushers Gretchen Hailer	$5.95
Lights in the Darkness Ave Clark, O.P.	$8.95
Loving Yourself for God's Sake Adolfo Quezada	$5.95
Mother Teresa Eugene Palumbo	$5.95
Personally Speaking Jim Lisante	$8.95
Practicing the Prayer of Presence van Kaam/Muto	$8.95
5-Minute Miracles Linda Schubert	$4.95
Season of New Beginnings Mitch Finley	$4.95
Season of Promises Mitch Finley	$4.95
Stay with Us John Mullin, SJ	$3.95
Surprising Mary Mitch Finley	$7.95
Teaching as Eucharist Joanmarie Smith	$5.95
What He Did for Love Francis X. Gaeta	$5.95
You Are My Beloved Mitch Finley	$10.95
Your Sacred Story Robert Lauder	$6.95

For a free catalog call 1-800-892-6657